The Black Lives Matter Movement

Peggy J. Parks

ReferencePoint Press®

San Diego, CA

For more information, contact:
ReferencePoint Press, Inc.
PO Box 27779
San Diego, CA 92198
www.ReferencePointPress.com

LIBRARY OF CONGRESS CATALOGING-IN-PUBLICATION DATA

Names: Parks, Peggy J., 1951– author.
Title: The Black Lives Matter Movement/by Peggy J. Parks.
Description: San Diego, CA: ReferencePoint Press, [2017] | Audience: Grade 9
    to 12. | Includes bibliographical references and index. | Audience: Grades 9–12.
Identifiers: LCCN 2017023860 (print) | LCCN 2017030518 (ebook) | ISBN
    9781682822869 (eBook) | ISBN 9781682822852 (hardback)
Subjects: LCSH: Black lives matter movement. | African Americans—Civil
    rights. | United States—Race relations. | Racial profiling in law
    enforcement—United States. | African Americans—Social conditions—21st
    century. | Racism—United States.
Classification: LCC E185.615 (ebook) | LCC E185.615 .P337 2017 (print) | DDC
    323.1196/073—dc23
LC record available at https://lccn.loc.gov/2017023860

CONTENTS

Fighting for Equality

On July 13, 2013, in a packed courtroom in Sanford, Florida, a verdict sent shock waves through America's African American community. After two days of deliberation, a jury found George Zimmerman, a Sanford neighborhood watch volunteer, not guilty of second-degree murder in the shooting death of an unarmed black teenager named Trayvon Martin. When the verdict was announced, writer and community activist Alicia Garza was in a bar in Oakland, California, with her husband and some friends. They, as well as other patrons in the bar, had all been checking their phones regularly and read about the verdict on social media. When it was announced, everyone was stunned into silence. "Everything went quiet,"[1] says Garza. Then, she says, everyone in the bar started getting out of their seats and leaving all at once.

As the bar emptied out, Garza was struck by how beaten down all the people appeared to be. "It was like we couldn't look at each other," she says. "We were carrying this burden around with us every day: of racism and white supremacy. It was a verdict that said: black people are not safe in America."[2] Filled with despair, Garza went home with her husband and cried for much of the evening.

From Defeat to Empowerment

The next day Garza woke up with a sense of urgency—she felt compelled to reach out to her fellow African Americans. She composed a Facebook post that she calls "a love letter to black people." In the post, Garza expressed her despair at knowing that many people cheered the Zimmerman verdict, believing it to be cause for celebration. "That makes me sick to my stomach," she wrote. "We GOTTA get it together y'all." Later, feeling a bit more energized, she added to her post. "I continue to be surprised at how little Black lives matter," she wrote. "And I will continue that. Stop giving up on black life. . . . Black people. I love you. I love us. Our lives matter."[3]

As soon as the post appeared on Facebook, it started attracting attention. Garza's close friend, Patrisse Cullors, saw it and was inspired by the message. She shared it with her Facebook friends and added the hashtag #BlackLivesMatter at the end of her post. On the other side of the country, in New York City, immigration rights organizer Opal Tometi saw the post and was captivated by the hashtag.

> "Stop giving up on black life. . . . Black people. I love you. I love us. Our lives matter."[3]
>
> —Alicia Garza, cofounder of Black Lives Matter

She instinctively knew it represented something important, and she contacted Garza, whom she had previously met while doing civil rights work. Tometi volunteered to build a digital platform for Black Lives Matter on social media. Tometi, Garza, and Cullors then talked about how they could use the Black Lives Matter slogan to launch not only a social media presence, but a whole new civil rights movement. "We wanted to connect people who were already buzzing about all this stuff and get them to do something, not just retweet or like or share," says Garza. "We thought, How do we get folks together and take that energy and create something awesome?"[4]

The three women passionately believed in the cause because of their own personal experience with racism. Also, they had observed numerous situations in which they felt law enforcement had unfairly targeted African Americans. They were ready to get to work on building a movement that could bring people of color together to help make a positive difference. "To make sure we are creating a world where black lives actually do matter,"[5] says Garza.

Growth and Growing Pains

In the years since the Black Lives Matter movement was launched, it has grown and changed significantly. Today it is a network of

Protesters march across the street from the federal courthouse in Brooklyn, New York, in 2015. The Black Lives Matter movement began as a Facebook post and then blossomed into a nationwide campaign to bring about change in US policing and race relations.

more than forty chapters in cities throughout the United States. Each of these chapters operates autonomously and does its own work on behalf of civil rights. As awareness of the movement has grown, a number of influential people have spoken out to express their support for Black Lives Matter. These include musician superstars Lady Gaga, Rihanna, Beyoncé and her husband Jay

Z, and rapper Kendrick Lamar; Facebook founder Mark Zuckerberg; pro basketball stars LeBron James, Carmelo Anthony, and Dwyane Wade; actress Kerry Washington; tennis great Serena Williams; and reality television star Kim Kardashian West, among a host of others.

Black Lives Matter also has its share of detractors. Many who object to the movement take issue with an organization specifically devoted to the rights of African Americans, alleging that all lives matter, not only black lives. The movement's harsh criticism of police officers who abuse their authority has been blamed for several brutal slayings of police officers. These killings have led to a fringe movement called Blue Lives Matter. In a July 2016 televised address, then-president Barack Obama addressed concerns about the movement, saying that the purpose of Black Lives Matter was never to place a higher value on black people's lives than any other lives, including those of police officers. The point of the movement, he explained, is to emphasize that black lives matter *equally*. "This isn't a matter of us comparing the value of lives," Obama said. "This is recognizing that there is a particular burden that is being placed on a group of our fellow citizens, and we should care about that—and we can't dismiss it."[6]

As civil rights leaders, activists, and supporters look toward the future, they are well aware that they face many challenges. They believe that racism remains a formidable problem in the United States but know that not everyone is convinced of that. There continue to be clashes between Black Lives Matter activists and those who do not support the movement. And incidents of police discrimination and brutality continue to occur.

> **"This movement, largely driven by young people, is really the civil and human rights struggle of our time."[7]**
>
> —Barbara Lee, a US representative from Oakland, California

Yet despite the challenges, supporters believe that Black Lives Matter can make a positive difference for African Americans and for society as a whole. One ardent supporter, California representative Barbara Lee, says that what Garza, Cullors, and Tometi collectively founded will be successful at driving change. "This movement," says Lee, "largely driven by young people, is really the civil and human rights struggle of our time."[7]

7

CHAPTER ONE

The Dangerous Divide Between Black Citizens and Police

The founders of Black Lives Matter were guided by a vision: a world in which black people's lives are valued as much as the lives of white people. From what they had personally experienced in their own lives, the founders had concluded that black and white lives were not at all valued equally. On an ongoing basis, they lived through and witnessed what they saw as society's unrelenting devaluation of black people's lives. To Alicia Garza, Patrisse Cullors, Opal Tometi, and everyone else who is part of this new civil rights movement, the acquittal of Trayvon Martin's killer was just one more example of a black life that did not matter.

For many African Americans, nowhere is inequality more evident than in how they are treated by police officers. Although law enforcement's job is to keep people and communities safe, black citizens often feel threatened by police, rather than feeling protected. Over the long term, this has created a serious, volatile, and dangerous divide between black communities and police, whose job it is to maintain law and order. "We are not criminals because we are black," says *New York Times* investigative journalist Nikole Hannah-Jones. "Nor are we somehow the only people in America who don't want to live in safe neighborhoods. Yet many of us cannot fundamentally trust the people who are charged with keeping us and our communities safe." Hannah-Jones refers to the "gaping divide between law enforcement and the black communities they are supposed to serve."[8]

Deep-Seated Mistrust

A major contributor to this divide, says Hannah-Jones, is that black people are accustomed to being mistreated by police. As a result of this experience, they have little expectation of being treated fairly. Hannah-Jones has seen police officers treat black crime witnesses with suspicion, assuming they are suspects. Black professionals she knows have had guns drawn on them by police for no apparent reason. She has a lifetime of such experiences, which have collectively fueled her belief that law enforcement is not to be trusted.

One of these experiences occurred in July 2014, when Hannah-Jones and her family were celebrating the July Fourth holiday at Long Island, New York. After dinner she, her family, and some friends all went for a walk along the seashore. Everyone was in the holiday spirit and the mood was festive, with children laughing as they chased each other along the boardwalk. Suddenly, the carefree happiness of the day was shattered by gunshots. A young man on the street parallel to the boardwalk was shooting, and people began screaming and running toward the shoreline. Then, as quickly as it began, the gunfire stopped and the shooter ran away. A high school girl named Hunter, who was staying with Hannah-Jones and her family, called the police on her cell phone. Upon learning this, says Hannah-Jones, she and her friends were stunned and silent. "Between the four adults, we hold six degrees," she says. "Three of us are journalists. And not one of us had thought to call the police. We had not even considered it."[9]

Hunter's conversation with the police proved to be frightening rather than reassuring. Although she explained that she was only sixteen and from a different area, the officer seemed highly suspicious. As she stood on the boardwalk, the police called her back four times, supposedly to gather more information, and Hunter began to feel like a suspect. On one of the calls, the officer asked if Hunter was really trying to be helpful or if she had been involved in the shooting. This terrified the girl and made her wonder whether

> "We are not criminals because we are black. . . . Yet many of us cannot fundamentally trust the people who are charged with keeping us and our communities safe."[8]
>
> —*New York Times* investigative journalist Nikole Hannah-Jones

the police were coming to get her. To help lighten the mood, one of the people in the group made a joke about this being why they never call police. "We all laughed," says Hannah-Jones, "but it was hollow."[10]

Racial Profiling

One of the main reasons so many black people do not trust law enforcement is its use of tactics they see as discriminatory. They say, for instance, that black people are often stopped and questioned by police for no apparent reason, other than the color of their skin. This is known as racial profiling, which involves being suspicious of people solely on the basis of race, ethnicity, religion, or national origin. "Racial profiling," says the American Civil Liberties Union (ACLU), "is a longstanding and deeply troubling national problem despite claims that the United States has entered a 'post-racial era.'"[11]

> "Racial profiling is a longstanding and deeply troubling national problem despite claims that the United States has entered a 'post-racial era.'"[11]
>
> —ACLU, which fights to defend and preserve constitutional rights

Racial profiling is illegal because it violates the US Constitution's guarantee of equal protection under the law and freedom from unreasonable searches. Still, the African American community and civil rights activists point to evidence showing that profiling remains a common practice. "It occurs every day, in cities and towns across the country," says the ACLU, "when law enforcement and private security target people of color for humiliating and often frightening detentions, interrogations, and searches without evidence of criminal activity."[12] The perception among blacks that racial profiling is prevalent was revealed during a 2016 survey conducted by the Black Youth Project. The survey involved nearly two thousand young adults aged eighteen to thirty. The majority of participants agreed that police do not treat all ethnic groups equally. When asked if they trust police to do what is right, only about one-quarter of African Americans said yes, compared with three-quarters of white participants.

In communities where racial profiling appears to be common, black drivers are stopped by police far more often than are white

Police officers stop a young African American man in San Francisco. Police in that Northern California city have been accused of stopping, searching, and arresting blacks far more often than whites.

drivers. Black people familiar with this experience use the slang term "driving while black" to describe it. "The cops want to pull you over, so they pull you over," says Caleb Roberts, a young black graduate student from Milwaukee, Wisconsin. "They don't need a reason. They can make up a reason. And they will, especially if you're Black."[13]

Roberts has personal experience to back up his assertion. When he was eighteen and driving home from a concert with some friends in the car, Roberts passed two police cars headed in the opposite direction. "In that moment," he says, "I felt that familiar spike of worry that most young black men feel when they encounter the police. But I quickly convinced myself it was nothing." Suddenly, both cruisers made an abrupt U-turn. With sirens wailing and lights flashing, they raced up behind Roberts and pulled him over. Four officers got out of the cars and headed toward him with their guns drawn. "I was being treated like a criminal for no reason," says Roberts. One officer opened the driver's side door and demanded that Roberts put his hands on the steering wheel. The other officers opened the passenger doors and made his friends get out and wait while their driver's licenses were checked for outstanding warrants. "None of it felt right," says Roberts. "We were young people coming home from a concert. And we were terrified."[14]

> "The cops want to pull you over, so they pull you over. They don't need a reason. They can make up a reason."[13]
>
> —Caleb Roberts, an African American graduate student from Milwaukee, Wisconsin

Another black man who believes he was singled out because of his race is Jerard Jack, a former military police officer with the US Army. Jack, who is from Lake Charles, Louisiana, was on his way to visit his grandmother, who had been hospitalized. A police officer pulled him over, saying that Jack resembled a crime suspect. When Jack questioned this contention, the officer began cursing at him and threatened him with a stun gun. Another policeman, who was a friend of Jack's, was driving by and pulled over to see what the problem was. He persuaded the first officer to let Jack go. Jack then drove to the hospital, where he learned that his grandmother had died.

Unfair and Unlawful

Numerous investigations have shown that black people throughout the United States have had such run-ins with the police. During the 2016 Black Youth Project survey, 28 percent of young black adults said they had been arrested after encounters with law enforcement. When asked if they had been personally harassed by police, 24 percent of blacks said they had, compared with 8 percent of whites. More than half of black respondents reported knowing someone who had been arrested and/or harassed by police.

One city that has received many complaints of racial profiling is San Francisco, California. A report released in July 2016 exam-

The Tragic Death of Tamir Rice

On November 22, 2014, a man in Cleveland, Ohio, called 911 to report something he had observed in a park. He told the dispatcher that a young male was pointing a pistol at people to scare them, although he said it was probably a fake weapon. The boy was Tamir Rice, a black twelve-year-old who was playing with a pellet gun he had borrowed from a friend. Police were dispatched to the scene—but were never told that the suspect was likely a child with a fake gun.

Officers raced to the park and drove over a curb, stopping just a few feet from Tamir. They jumped out of the car with guns drawn. Thinking that the boy was reaching for the pistol in his waistband, Officer Timothy Loehmann fired twice at close range, striking Tamir in the abdomen. The boy fell facedown onto the snow-covered grass, and neither officer administered first aid. About four minutes later an FBI agent who was in the area stopped to assist. He cared for Tamir until an ambulance arrived to transport the boy to the hospital. Tamir died at the hospital the following day. An investigation cleared Loehmann of criminal charges, although he and the dispatcher, who had failed to tell officers that the boy's gun might be fake, faced disciplinary action. Tamir's family was convinced that the boy's shooting was another example of how little police value black lives, even the life of a child. According to prosecutor Timothy J. McGinty, however, the officer had shot the boy because he genuinely feared for his life. Tamir's shooting, he said, was terrible and tragic but it was not a crime.

ined police practices in the city. It shows that black people were far more likely than whites to be stopped by police, searched, and arrested. Especially prevalent among black drivers was unwarranted search. Whereas 1.7 percent of whites were searched during a traffic stop, more than 13 percent of black drivers were subjected to such searches.

According to a 2015 investigation by the US Department of Justice (DOJ), racial profiling is also a serious problem in Ferguson, Missouri, a suburb of St. Louis. The study revealed that officers consistently practiced "unconstitutional policing." Police were found to be generating revenue for the city by targeting black residents with frivolous infractions and levying expensive fines. Citizens were being stopped and often searched without reasonable suspicion and arrested without probable cause, both of which violate the Constitution's Fourth Amendment. Officers were using unreasonable force against citizens, which is another violation of the Fourth Amendment. And they were also interfering with citizens' right to free speech, which is in violation of the First Amendment. "Many officers appear to see some residents, especially those who live in Ferguson's predominantly African-American neighborhoods, less as constituents to be protected than as potential offenders and sources of revenue,"[15] the report authors wrote.

Protesters in Washington, DC, hold up their hands in a symbolic gesture that means: "Don't shoot." This gesture has been repeated at many Black Lives Matter protests to show solidarity with victims who had tried to show police that they were unarmed.

During its investigation, the DOJ uncovered many troubling incidents in which black citizens of Ferguson were victims of police misconduct. One of these took place during the summer of 2012. On a hot, humid day, a thirty-two-year-old black man named Michael was sitting in his car cooling off after playing basketball in a park. A police officer pulled up behind his car and blocked him in. The officer approached Michael and accused him of preying on little children in the park. After being ordered to produce his identification and Social Security number, Michael was told to get out of the car to be patted down and searched. When Michael protested, saying his constitutional rights were being violated, the officer pulled out his gun and arrested him. Michael was charged with eight violations of Ferguson's municipal code, including making a false declaration, because Michael initially said his name was Mike. Another charge, says the DOJ report, was for not wearing a seat belt even though Michael was sitting in a parked car.

The Shooting Death of Michael Brown

The DOJ's investigation of law enforcement in Ferguson was triggered by an August 9, 2014, incident in the city. Michael Brown Jr., a black eighteen-year-old, was shot and killed by a white police officer named Darren Wilson. Brown and a friend had been walking in the street when Wilson drove by and yelled at them to get on the sidewalk. The young men refused. Exact details of what happened next are murky, although it is known that Brown and Wilson had a scuffle at the police car, which resulted in Brown getting shot in the hand. He and his friend, Dorian Johnson, took off running, with Wilson in pursuit. Brown then turned around and ran the other way while Johnson hid behind a car. Wilson started shooting at Brown, striking him at least six times. The officer later said that he fired in self-defense because Brown was running toward him ready to attack.

A different account was presented by witnesses to the incident. According to Johnson, Wilson began firing the second Brown tried to run away. "I saw the officer proceeding after my friend Big Mike with his gun drawn, and he fired a second shot and that struck my friend," says Johnson. "And at that time, he turned around with his hands up, beginning to tell the officer that he was unarmed and to tell him to stop shooting. But at that time, the officer fired several more shots into my friend, and he hit the ground and died."[16]

15

After the shooting, Brown's body lay facedown in the middle of the street, where it remained for at least four hours. Patricia Bynes, an African American council member from Ferguson, is convinced that the delay in removing the young man's body was an intentional sign of disrespect. "It sent . . . the message from law enforcement that 'we can do this to you any day, any time, in broad daylight, and there's nothing you can do about it,'"[17] says Bynes. Yet not everyone perceived the delay in removing Brown's body as an intentional slight. Police officers say that many factors were involved, and not all were within law enforcement's control. Still, in the wake of Brown's death, many officials have said it was inexcusable that such a long time lapsed before Brown's body was removed.

Police Killings

Brown's death proved to be the catalyst for a national debate on excessive use of force by law enforcement. It brought attention to police actions, specifically firearm deaths by police officers. According to investigations by the *Washington Post*, 991 people in the United States were shot to death by police officers in 2015; in 2016 the number dropped slightly to 957 deaths.

In both 2015 and 2016, the *Post* investigation found that a disproportionate number of people who were killed by police were black. Actual numbers show that police killed more white males than black males. But when the numbers were adjusted to account for the fact that there are far more whites than blacks in the US population, black males were found to be three times as likely to be killed by police. An even greater discrepancy was observed when examining armed versus unarmed shooting victims. The *Post* investigation found that more than 80 percent of the shooting victims were armed, most often with a gun or knife. Of the unarmed victims, a far greater percentage of black unarmed citizens were killed than were unarmed whites. One notable difference between the findings of 2015 and 2016 was that in the latter year, more of the fatal shootings were captured on video.

Caught on Camera

A September 2016 police killing of an unarmed black man was captured on video taken by a police helicopter. Forty-year-old Terence Crutcher had stopped his sport-utility vehicle on a two-lane road in Tulsa, Oklahoma. For reasons that are unknown, he walked away from the vehicle, leaving the engine running and the driver's side door open. Police officer Betty Shelby stopped to investigate and was soon joined by other officers. Shelby noticed Crutcher wandering around and asked him if the car was his vehicle, to which he mumbled a response she could not understand.

Shelby concluded that Crutcher was on drugs and posed a threat to her. With her weapon drawn, she commanded him to take his hands out of his pockets, which he did. He then began walking away from her with his hands in the air. Video footage shows Shelby and the other officers with their guns trained on

Tulsa, Oklahoma police officer Betty Shelby arrives for her arraignment after being charged with manslaughter in the death of Terence Crutcher in 2016. In 2017 a jury found Shelby not guilty of the crime.

"The Talk"

Wesley Lowery is a highly respected black journalist who writes for the *Washington Post*. He grew up in Cleveland, Ohio, a city that the DOJ has investigated for violating its residents' civil rights. As a black teenager, Lowery says that he and his friends had their "fair share of colourful interactions" with Cleveland police. Nearly all the boys had a conversation with their parents or another adult that Lowery refers to as "the talk." He says, "Find almost any high school-age black male and ask him about 'the talk.'"

During this very serious conversation, the message that is passed along to black youths is one of self-awareness. Parents stress that because of their children's skin color, many people—especially the police—tend to view them not only as less important than white people but also as a threat to white people. The teens are instructed to say "yes sir" and "yes ma'am" to any police officer they encounter. If they are driving and get pulled over, they must keep their hands on the wheel so they are not assumed to be reaching for a weapon. Lowery and his friends always kept their wallets in the center console of any vehicle they were riding in. By doing so, if they were pulled over, they would never have to reach into their pockets—again, so as to not be perceived as threatening. "Above all," says Lowery, "we knew to never, ever run in the presence of a police officer. That's just asking for trouble."

Wesley Lowery, "Black Lives Matter: Birth of a Movement," *Guardian* (Manchester), January 17, 2017. www.theguardian.com.

Crutcher as he walked toward his vehicle. Suddenly, he dropped to the ground and blood began seeping through his white T-shirt. Shelby had shot him. She later claimed that she did so because she feared that Crutcher was headed to his vehicle to get a weapon. Crutcher was transported to the hospital, where he was pronounced dead. A later search of his vehicle found a vial of the drug PCP but no weapons of any kind. Shelby was indicted for first-degree manslaughter. On May 18, 2017, after nine hours of deliberation, a jury of eight women and four men, including three African Americans, found Shelby not guilty.

Another unarmed black man whose killing was caught on videotape was Walter Scott, who was a veteran of the US Coast

Guard. In April 2015 Scott was pulled over by a white police officer named Michael Slager, who stopped Scott for a broken taillight. There was some kind of scuffle outside the vehicle, and Slager shot Scott. Slager later claimed that the shooting was in self-defense, saying that Scott had threatened him and tried to get his stun gun. A three-minute video taken by a bystander, however, shows something quite different. In the video Scott can be seen running away from Slager, who then shoots Scott in the back at least eight times as he tries to flee. "If it were not for the video," says journalist James E. Causey, "then we would be forced to take the officer's word for what happened, and the case would simply go down as another black man who was shot and killed by police after a violent altercation."[18] In May 2017 Slager pleaded guilty to one federal charge of violating Scott's civil rights. He was awaiting sentencing.

Causey, who is African American, says that Scott's violent death, as shown in the video, was sickening. "It opens a lot of old wounds," says Causey. "The fact that a black life can be brushed off like it's nothing is the main reason the campaign 'Black Lives Matter' has so much traction."[19] He goes on to say that police brutality, including shootings of unarmed people, is indicative of why black people in the United States do not trust and often fear police officers. This lack of trust between black citizens and the police, this dangerous divide, continues to spur Black Lives Matter activists to action.

> "The fact that a black life can be brushed off like it's nothing is the main reason the campaign 'Black Lives Matter' has so much traction."[19]
>
> —James E. Causey, a journalist from Milwaukee, Wisconsin

CHAPTER TWO

The Formation of a Movement

Although the Black Lives Matter name was coined in 2013, it was Michael Brown's death the following year that propelled a name and a hashtag into a full-fledged civil rights movement. On August 9, 2014, immediately after Brown was killed, gruesome images of his body lying in the Ferguson, Missouri, road raced through social media. It started with the St. Louis rapper Tef Poe, who tweeted a photo of Brown with the text: "The life less body of the unarmed 17 year old kid please help us expose this attempted cover."[20] Poe's photo was retweeted nearly fifty-three hundred times, and others at the scene were also tweeting details of Brown's killing. This widespread publicity sparked public outrage and captured the media's attention.

A group of activists, including Alicia Garza, Patrisse Cullors, and Opal Tometi, along with writer and activist Darnell Moore, coordinated what they called "freedom rides" to Missouri. People flocked to Ferguson from cities all over the United States, including New York; Chicago, Illinois; Portland, Oregon; Los Angeles, California; and Boston, Massachusetts. When Garza arrived, she was startled to see that many people carried signs or wore shirts emblazoned with "Black Lives Matter" and were shouting the slogan as they marched in support of Brown. Journalist and historian Jelani Cobb writes, "Within a few weeks of Brown's death, hundreds of people who had never participated in organized protests took to the streets." The result of that collective effort, says Cobb, was to expose Ferguson "as a case study of structural racism in America and a metaphor for all that had gone wrong since the end of the civil-rights movement."[21]

Spotlight on Racism

In using the term *structural racism*, Cobb is referring to a societal system in which Caucasians are assumed to be superior to other races. In such a system, which many are convinced exists in the United States, white people are afforded more advantages and privileges than people of color. Sociologists Keith Lawrence and Terry Keleher write, "It is a system of hierarchy and inequity, primarily characterized by white supremacy—the preferential treatment, privilege and power for white people at the expense of Black, Latino, Asian, Pacific Islander, Native American, Arab and other racially oppressed people."[22] One of the most important goals of the Black Lives Matter movement is building awareness of how pervasive racism is in American society. Activists have found that to be a challenging task, however, as white people often deny that racism is much of a problem.

> "Within a few weeks of Brown's death, hundreds of people who had never participated in organized protests took to the streets."[21]
>
> —Jelani Cobb, a journalist and historian from New York City

The most threatening examples of racism are the instances where racial profiling is known to occur and when relationships between people of color and law enforcement are volatile. But, activists say, there are numerous examples of racism that are not always so obvious. On a day-to-day basis, people of color are victims of discriminatory treatment that affects every aspect of their lives yet rarely makes news headlines. One family for whom racism is a near-constant source of stress, frustration, and fear is the Waters family from Dallas, Texas. The family lives in a wealthy North Dallas neighborhood. Both parents (Frances and James) are attorneys, and they are highly respected in their community. Yet they constantly face racism in their daily lives.

One disturbing occurrence was when Frances Waters was in a neighborhood bookstore shopping for a geography book for her son. She noticed that a store employee was following her and continued to do so wherever Frances moved throughout the store. The same thing happened on another occasion. That time, Frances became so frustrated at being shadowed that she returned several hundred dollars' worth of books she had purchased and ordered the books online instead. "I guess they think

I'm very dangerous, right?" she asks. Despite the fact that she is an attorney, as well as pastor of the family's church, "all they see is black,"[23] she says. Black people throughout the United States share her frustration, and for many, Black Lives Matter offers hope that things will get better.

A New Generation of Activists

The Black Lives Matter movement evolved in a loose, largely unplanned way. The name was a natural outgrowth of the #BlackLivesMatter hashtag that was created by Garza, Cullors, and Tometi. But the movement itself, fueled by outrage over Brown's death and the exoneration of his killer, was started by young, passionate civil rights activists from all over America. Referring to the movement as a "decentralized collection of grass-roots activists and groups," journalist Josh Hafner describes how it came together: through the actions of Black Lives Matter protesters who "rallied on the streets of cities around the nation where African Americans have been killed in police-involved shootings."[24]

Black Lives Matter does not have a well-defined hierarchy or clear leaders. As a result, the movement has sometimes been criticized for lacking structure and focus. One critic was Oprah Winfrey, who said in a 2015 interview, "I think it's wonderful to march and to protest and it's wonderful to see all across the country, people doing it." Winfrey added, however, that marching alone is not enough. "What I'm looking for," she said, "is some kind of leadership to come out of this to say, 'This is what we want. This is what has to change, and these are the steps that we need to take to make these changes, and this is what we're willing to do to get it.'"[25] Yet the young activists who have emerged as Black Lives Matter leaders take issue with anyone saying that the movement lacks leadership. They emphasize that not being under the leadership of just one or two people enables a decentralized approach, with many activists pursuing change in the way they believe to be most beneficial.

Young, Passionate, and Highly Motivated for Change

Among the most visible, and vocal, of the Black Lives Matter activists is a young black woman from St. Louis, Missouri, named

Johnetta Elzie. She grew up not far from where Brown was killed, and she now lives about two hours away. When she read about his death on Twitter, she drove to the scene where his body had lain in the street. "His body was gone but the blood was still there,"[26] says Elzie. Overcome with emotion, she was determined to get the message out to people to make them aware of what happened. She began live-tweeting from Ferguson and became one of the most prolific documenters of the murky details surrounding Brown's death.

Through her involvement with what she calls "The Movement," Elzie became close friends with another young black activist, a former school administrator from Minneapolis, Minnesota, named DeRay Mckesson. In mid-August 2014, a week after Brown's death, Mckesson drove nine hours from his home in Minneapolis to Ferguson, where he met other activists, including Elzie. He shared her outrage over the injustice of Brown's killing as well as the high prevalence of black citizens who had been killed by

Activists DeRay Mckesson and Johnetta Elzie (both pictured) are among the most visible and vocal members of the Black Lives Matter movement. Both have sought to bring attention to police shootings of African Americans.

A Most Daring Feat

Black Lives Matter is made up of people from cities and towns throughout the United States. The movement is relatively unstructured; activists have the freedom to pursue their own civil rights actions however they see fit. This is exactly what thirty-year-old Brittany "Bree" Newsome did in 2015. The Confederate flag, which for many people represents pre–Civil War white supremacy and slavery, had flown for years on the grounds of the South Carolina state capitol building in Columbia. Frustrated over the lack of action to remove what she saw as a derogatory symbol, Newsome decided to do it herself.

On June 27, 2015, at five thirty in the morning, Newsome arrived at the capitol building dressed in full climbing gear and wearing a helmet. With police and other onlookers watching, she shimmied up the 30-foot (9.14-m) flagpole and removed the flag; immediately, photos of the bold undertaking began appearing on Twitter under the #BlackLivesMatter hashtag. When Newsome returned to the ground with the flag in hand, she was promptly arrested. Smiling brightly, she was led away in handcuffs to jail. She quickly became a social media hero, with celebrities, politicians, and civil rights activists tweeting their support for her under the hashtag #FreeBree. In her public statement, Newsome said: "We can't wait any longer. We can't continue like this another day. It's time for a new chapter where we are sincere about dismantling white supremacy and building toward true racial justice and equality." The charges against Newsome were dropped, and two weeks after her arrest, the South Carolina Legislature voted to remove the flag.

Quoted in Greg Botelho and Emanuella Gringerg, "Bree Newsome Hailed for Removing Confederate Flag," CNN, June 27, 2015. www.cnn.com.

police across the nation. Mckesson joined Elzie in live-tweeting what was taking place in Ferguson. A few days later he went back to Minneapolis but continued to return to Ferguson, making the 600-mile (966-km) commute every weekend. Finally, he quit his job to become a full-time activist and lived off money he had been saving. In a short time he and Elzie became well known for their involvement with Black Lives Matter.

Along with Mckesson and Elzie, a young black woman named Brittany Packnett has also become a prominent Black Lives Matter leader. Like Elzie, Packnett grew up in St. Louis, and she also took part in demonstrations after Michael Brown's killing. She says his death deepened her commitment to social justice. "It is about defending the humanity and the dignity of all people in this country and of people of color in particular,"[27] she says. Packnett is an educator, writer, and public speaker, as well as an activist. When then-president Barack Obama formed the Task Force on 21st Century Policing, he asked Packnett to be a part of it, and she accepted. Along with Mckesson, Elzie, and an activist named Samuel Sinyangwe, Packnett cofounded Campaign Zero, a reform campaign that aims to reduce police violence.

> "People would not have heard about Ferguson if it wasn't for social media. And when I say social media, I mean Twitter."[29]
>
> —Samuel Sinyangwe, a data scientist and analyst who is active in Black Lives Matter

Sinyangwe is another emerging leader in the Black Lives Matter movement. He grew up in Orlando, Florida, and as a boy attended soccer practice just a short distance from where Trayvon Martin was shot. "I used to go to that same 7/11 [as Martin] every day for a packet of Starburst," says Sinyangwe. "It could have been me. It really could have been anyone who looked like me."[28] When he heard about Michael Brown's shooting, Sinyangwe felt much the same as other black activists: that Brown should not have been killed, that his death was an injustice. Sinyangwe began following Mckesson's live-tweeting from Ferguson, and the two began talking via social media and on the phone.

Growth Fueled by Social Media

Sinyangwe, who graduated from Stanford University, is a data scientist and policy analyst. He emphasizes the invaluable role that social media has played in the widespread recognition of Black Lives Matter. "People would not have heard about Ferguson if it wasn't for social media," he says. "And when I say social media, I mean Twitter." Beyond public awareness, social media has been a powerful force in the growth of the movement. "It allows people to organize and build a community where it previously has not been,"[29] says Sinyangwe. After the #BlackLivesMatter hashtag first appeared on social media in July 2013, its use grew and then declined sharply by July 2014. But according to a Center

Brittany Packnett attends a White House meeting with President Barack Obama in 2016. Packnett cofounded Campaign Zero, a reform effort that aims to reduce violence by police, especially against people of color.

for Media & Social Impact study, Brown's death in August caused the hashtag's use to soar to 52,288 tweets that month. The study determined that Brown's killing, together with the widespread protests and subsequent media publicity, launched Black Lives Matter from a slogan and hashtag to a national movement. Tens of millions of tweets have appeared with the #BlackLivesMatter hashtag.

All Black Lives Matter activists have been involved in social media, but Mckesson has emerged as the movement's social media leader. Packnett explains why, of the many people tweeting and posting images from the protests in Ferguson, Mckesson stood out more than anyone. "DeRay is really adept at telling very

A Future Civil Rights Leader

He is only eighteen years old, but Ziad Ahmed is already determined to be an activist for social justice. Ahmed is not black; he is Muslim American. But he refers to himself as "an unapologetic progressive activist" who is a strong advocate of the Black Lives Matter movement. He is so devoted to the movement, in fact, that he used it as a focal point while filling out his application to Stanford University. In response to a question about what matters most to him and why, Ahmed wrote "#BlackLivesMatter" exactly one hundred times. He says he wanted the admissions officers to truly understand his "impatience for justice and the significance of it." He explains: "The hashtag conveys my frustration with the failure of [the] judicial system to protect the black community from violence, systemic inequity, and political disenfranchisement."

Ahmed was accepted to Stanford, as well as Yale and Princeton Universities. Whatever his future holds, he plans to use his voice to help bring about positive change and do all he can to help end racism.

Quoted in Avalon Zoppo, "Teen Accepted to Stanford After Writing #BlackLivesMatter 100 Times on Application," NBC News, April 5, 2017. www.nbcnews.com.

succinct stories," she says, "so it'd be, 'I'm running from tear gas #Ferguson' or 'I have to sleep under my steering wheel to get away from the police #Ferguson.' There is something clear and sharp about his language that really speaks to a lot of people."[30]

Mckesson is a constant presence on Twitter, with nearly eight hundred thousand followers as of May 2017. He posts regularly about social justice issues, denouncing police who have been accused of killings or brutality. He is openly critical of law enforcement tactics that are unfair and unjust to black citizens. He speaks out against government decisions that erode people's civil rights. And as Mckesson continues to express his strong opinions through tweets, his followers keep growing—including those who hate him, as well as those who love and admire him. In a December 2015 CNN article, journalists Sara Sidner and Mallory Simon write, "He's been called everything from the new Martin Luther King Jr. to a devil intent on dividing America, depending on who is responding to him."[31]

Reporting the Truth

For Black Lives Matter activists, one unique and important advantage of social media is the ability to report news in real time, exactly as it is happening, and also to correct misconceptions and report errors—and outright falsehoods. Sometimes activists have tweeted information that conflicts with what the mainstream media are saying, as well as claims made by law enforcement.

According to Steven Pargett, who is with the social justice group Dream Defenders, during the Ferguson protests activists used Twitter to point out contradictions between police reports and what eyewitnesses were actually seeing. For example, while television networks were focused on reporting about rioting and looting, activists were tweeting about the disproportionate show of force by police. The police arrived in armored vehicles, used military-grade equipment, and fired tear gas and rubber bullets into crowds of people who were protesting peacefully.

> "[DeRay Mckesson]'s been called everything from the new Martin Luther King Jr. to a devil intent on dividing America, depending on who is responding to him."[31]
>
> —Sara Sidner and Mallory Simon, CNN journalists

The authors of a 2016 study called *Beyond the Hashtags* write: "We saw no examples of highly-retweeted eyewitness accounts supporting the police response."[32]

Disharmony on Display

As immensely valuable as social media has been to the growth of Black Lives Matter, it also allows the public to witness rivalry and, at times, hostile interactions between movement leaders. "Disagreements about tactics are totally normal," says Cullors. "We have differing opinions. This happened during the 60s in the days of Martin Luther King, and the Black Panther movement. It is just that our disagreements are often displayed to the public in real time on social media."[33] As normal as such conflicts may be, Cullors worries that infighting could be destructive and detract from the important work that needs to be done.

On more than one occasion, conflicts have arisen on Twitter between Elzie and Garza. Elzie does not hide her resentment that Garza, Cullors, and Tometi are credited with founding Black

Lives Matter. Even though they came up with the name and were the first to promote the hashtag on social media, Elzie says the movement was fueled by Brown's killing in Ferguson. Therefore, she considers that event to be the cradle of the Black Lives Matter movement. "In some ways," says Cobb, "it's an entity that has two births. It's conceived after one tragedy and really comes to fruition after another."[34]

In February 2016 a hostile exchange took place on Twitter. Garza had been asked to speak about Black Lives Matter at Webster University in St. Louis, and she had accepted. Upon learning about it, Elzie fired off an acrimonious tweet, saying that the notion of Garza being a founder of the movement was a lie and questioning why she should be the one to speak on behalf of the movement. Other tweets followed, with some threatening Garza with violence. She promptly canceled her scheduled appearance at Webster and tweeted that due to threats from "local activists with whom we have made an effort to have meaningful dialogue," she would not be speaking at the university. Her final tweet stated, "We all lose when bullying and personal attacks become a substitute for genuine conversation and principled disagreement."[35]

Moving Forward

In just a few years, Black Lives Matter has evolved from a small, grassroots activist group into a powerful, widely known social justice and civil rights movement. Many people have contributed to making this happen, from the three women who coined the name and created the hashtag, to other activists who were motivated to join by the summer 2014 protests in Ferguson, Missouri. Not everyone agrees on what the future of the movement should look like, but one thing is for sure: Black Lives Matter has captured the public's attention and made its presence known.

CHAPTER THREE

The Backlash

On Thursday, July 7, 2016, hundreds of Black Lives Matter activists marched in downtown Dallas, Texas. They had assembled to protest police killings of two black men earlier that week: thirty-seven-year-old Alton Sterling in Baton Rouge, Louisiana, and thirty-two-year-old Philando Castile near St. Paul, Minnesota. Neither of the men had brandished a weapon, but each was shot at close range by a police officer. In both cases a witness used a cell phone to record the sequence of events. Both officers faced criminal charges (In June 2017 a jury found the officer who shot Castile not guilty of second-degree manslaughter).

The protest in Dallas was well organized and moving along peacefully. Police Chief David O. Brown, who is black, had helped plan the event with some of his officers and Black Lives Matter organizers. About one hundred police officers were stationed along the route, and they walked along with the crowd. Some of them took the time to pose for selfies with demonstrators. The Dallas Police Department tweeted photos showing officers and demonstrators posing together and smiling at the camera. Jeff Hood, a white pastor and Black Lives Matter activist, later remarked that he was talking with a Dallas police department sergeant "about how peaceful and nonviolent the protest had been."[36] Suddenly, that peacefulness was shattered by the crack of gunshots. A sniper, heavily armed and perched on higher ground, had opened fire, and police officers were his target.

Assigning Blame

By the time the shooting stopped, five officers were dead and nine had been wounded, as were two civilians. The sniper was a twenty-five-year-old African American military veteran named Micah Xavier Johnson, who had served in Afghanistan with the US Army. After the shooting, Johnson fled to a nearby parking garage. Police negotiators surrounded the structure and tried to convince him to hand over his weapons and surrender, but Johnson refused. He was furious, he told them, over the recent police killings of black men, and he intended to avenge their deaths by hurting and killing white police officers. He asked how many officers he had killed and promised that more police deaths would be coming. Convinced that there was no other choice, the Dallas police bomb squad used a remote-control robot to kill Johnson with explosives. In a public statement, Brown said, "We're hurting. Our profession is hurting. . . . We are heartbroken. There are no words to describe the atrocity that occurred to our city. All I know is that this must stop, this divisiveness between our police and our citizens."[37]

> **"All I know is that this must stop, this divisiveness between our police and our citizens."[37]**
>
> —David O. Brown, Dallas, Texas, chief of police

Hood was in the middle of the terror and confusion during the shooting. He heard the shots and at first thought the noise had come from firecrackers—then he was sickened at the sight of police officers falling to the ground. "This is a devastating time for us as activists and organizers,"[38] he says. Although Hood was lead organizer of the Dallas protest, he stresses that justice will never be achieved through violence.

Because the shooting followed the Black Lives Matter protest, many people were convinced that Johnson was part of the movement. An investigation proved that to be false, however; Johnson had no association with Black Lives Matter. He was a deeply troubled individual, a reclusive loner who had been sent home from Afghanistan before his term was over. He was embittered over the shooting of blacks by white police officers, which motivated him to take revenge on them.

Immediately after the shooting, Black Lives Matter representatives condemned the act on social media and also published a statement on their website:

As we have done for decades, we marched and protested to highlight the urgent need to transform policing in America, to call for justice, transparency and accountability, and to demand that Black Lives Matter.

In Dallas, many gathered to do the same, joining in a day of action with friends, family, and co-workers. Their efforts were cut short when a lone gunman targeted and attacked 11 police officers, killing five. This is a tragedy—both for those who have been impacted by yesterday's attack and for our democracy.[39]

A Dallas resident offers her condolences and support at a makeshift memorial for five of the city's police officers who were gunned down by a sniper in 2016. The shootings occurred following a peaceful Black Lives Matter protest.

Yet for those who were convinced of Black Lives Matter's culpability, such statements were not enough. Even though representatives denounced the shooting, and despite Johnson having no involvement with the movement, many people still held the activists responsible. Critics claimed that the Black Lives Matter protests against police actions, combined with sensationalistic media coverage, had fanned the flames of antipolice sentiment. This, they said, had ultimately paved the way for the violent act.

In the wake of the shooting, one of the most outspoken critics of Black Lives Matter was Texas lieutenant governor Dan Patrick. In a July 8, 2016, interview with Fox News, Patrick said it was hypocritical for Black Lives Matter activists to march in protest of the police and then depend on those police to protect them. "All those protesters last night, they ran the other way expecting the

A New Hate Group

People who do not support Black Lives Matter have their own reasons for feeling the way they do. Some are turned off by the boisterous, confrontational approach of the protesters, while others misunderstand the movement's focus and assume it is a police-hating group. Many people object to the name, thinking "Black Lives Matter" implies that other lives matter less. As for the founders of a group called White Lives Matter, they object to Black Lives Matter because it promotes equality for black people. The group believes white people are superior to black people. "We have to do what ever possible to stem the rising tide of color," says White Lives Matter cofounder Doug Chism, "and acts of violence upon our people; we must try our best to take back our communities, we have to stand firm in the face of adversity, be rational, sensible and strong along the way."

Chism and his cofounders established White Lives Matter in direct response to Black Lives Matter. They are affiliated with known white supremacist organizations such as the Aryan Renaissance Society, National Socialist Movement, and Aryan National Alliance, among others. Because White Lives Matter is so openly hostile toward people of color and poses a significant threat to them, in August 2016 the Southern Poverty Law Center officially declared it to be a hate group.

Quoted in Southern Poverty Law Center, "White Lives Matter," 2017. www.splcenter.org.

men and women in blue to protect them," Patrick said. "What hypocrites! I understand the First Amendment. I understand freedom of speech. But you can't go out on social media and everywhere else and say the police are racist, the police are hateful, the police are killers."[40] Many like-minded individuals showed their support of Patrick on social media.

Lives Matter

Although animosity toward Black Lives Matter surged after the Dallas shootings, it actually began years before that. From the time the #BlackLivesMatter hashtag first appeared on Twitter, people began lashing out at the movement, with many condemning its very existence. One of the biggest complaints was the name; by singling out black lives, critics said, the implication was that they were worth more than nonblack lives. Rather than emphasizing that black lives matter, they said, the emphasis should be that *all* lives matter. Black Lives Matter cofounder Alicia Garza acknowledges that all lives matter—but she argues that people who bring that up are missing the point of what Black Lives Matter is about.

> "You can't go out on social media and everywhere else and say the police are racist, the police are hateful, the police are killers."[40]
>
> —Dan Patrick, lieutenant governor of Texas

"We live in a world where some lives matter more than others," says Garza. "'All Lives Matter' effectively neutralises the fact that it's black people who are fighting for their lives right now."[41]

Law enforcement professionals have had mixed reactions to Black Lives Matter. Many, such as the officers who were so supportive during the Dallas protest, are not troubled by the movement, nor are they bothered by the name. But others in law enforcement feel differently, viewing Black Lives Matter as hostile and antipolice, rather than antipolice *violence*. In August 2015, after a black man shot and killed a sheriff's deputy in Harris County, Texas, Sheriff Ron Hickman spoke out against Black Lives Matter. He condemned the "very dangerous national rhetoric" against police officers, which he said had spiraled out of control. Hickman stressed that the deputy's murder was in direct retaliation for shootings of black people by police officers. In a press conference, he said: "We heard 'black lives matter.' . . . Well, cops' lives matter too, so why don't we drop the qualifier and say 'lives matter.'"[42]

A number of active and retired law enforcement officers throughout the United States feel so negatively toward Black Lives Matter that they formed their own movement. Known as Blue Lives Matter, it was founded in 2014 in response to the nation-wide protest over Michael Brown's shooting death in Ferguson, Missouri. Writings on the Blue Lives Matter website express un-wavering support for Darren Wilson, Brown's shooter, saying that he "was forced to defend his life by shooting Brown." The website also denounces Black Lives Matter, claiming that its primary goal is to vilify law enforcement. The website claims that Black Lives Matter activists are "agitators" who spread lies about police of-ficers, namely "the absurd message that people were being shot by law enforcement simply because of the color of their skin."[43] According to Blue Lives Matter supporters, whenever people use the #BlueLivesMatter hashtag, they are showing their unwavering support of law enforcement.

Not everyone feels so positively about Blue Lives Matter. The group has been accused of being racist and uncondition-

Slain police officers are remembered at an event in Brooklyn, New York, in 2015. Law enforcement officers who were offended by the public profile of the Black Lives Matter movement began their own movement, known as Blue Lives Matter.

ally supportive of all law enforcement actions, even those that involve police brutality. According to Natasha Lennard, a news writer and political analyst, a Blue Lives Matter movement makes no sense because "there was never any doubt about the mattering of cops' lives in this country." She contrasts that with the dozens of unarmed black men killed every year, with little to no attention given to the loss of those lives. "That's what *not mattering* looks like in a society," she says. Lennard wants people to remember that Black Lives Matter was founded because black people have been, and are, oppressed by racism. Although police officers' lives absolutely do matter, and they are justified in being concerned for their lives, Lennard says "there remain no grounds at all to call police officers a persecuted minority, nor to equate the oppression of black life with that of police in America."[44]

> **"There remain no grounds at all to call police officers a persecuted minority, nor to equate the oppression of black life with that of police in America."[44]**
>
> —Natasha Lennard, a news writer and political analyst

Mixed Messages

One of the biggest complaints about Black Lives Matter is that it is anti–law enforcement. Even though activist leaders reject that viewpoint, insisting that it is false, the actions of some protesters suggest otherwise. One example is some of the signs displayed at many demonstrations, which have been openly hostile toward police officers. These signs use foul language and refer to officers by offensive names such "pigs" and "killers." At a 2016 rally in Irvine, California, protesters carried a large sign that said "Blue Lives Don't Matter." At some demonstrations, activists have yelled chants that vilify law enforcement and called for them to be harmed or killed. Such hostility has also been visible on social media, where posts and tweets have advocated revolt against police officers. In one tweet, an activist from Texas actually thanked Micah Xavier Johnson for the Dallas massacre of five police officers.

Black Lives Matter leaders have repeatedly said that these sorts of actions do not represent what the movement is about. They stress that changes are needed in the way law enforcement unfairly and unjustly targets black people, but they insist that the movement does not advocate violence. In fact, some demonstrations have been pro–law enforcement, such as one in Seattle, Washington, on July 22, 2016. Activists applauded the police who were on duty during the hours-long march. One protester said to a police officer standing nearby, "We don't hate you, we love you, we need you."[45] Some other protesters had similar positive remarks for the police on duty during the march.

Peniel Joseph, who teaches history at the University of Texas–Austin and is founder/director of the Center for the Study of Race and Democracy, emphasizes that Black Lives Matter has never been antipolice, antiwhite, or antigovernment. Rather, the thousands of people who have marched at demonstrations throughout the United States simply seek equality for black citizens. Blaming them for the violent deaths of police officers, says Joseph, obscures the important work that has been done since the movement began. He writes, "Black Lives Matter did not invent racial hatred or violence, but have instead mounted a human rights movement bold enough to articulate unspeakable, unspoken truths about a national culture of violence, division, and racial oppression."[46]

A Generation Gap

The type of human rights movement that Joseph describes is what Black Lives Matter envisions, and it is a goal shared by activists of all ages. Racial equality has been actively pursued by black citizens in the United States since the late Martin Luther King Jr. led freedom marches during the 1960s, when he gave his famous "I Have a Dream" speech. Yet many older civil rights activists who were part of that movement are not comfortable with Black Lives Matter.

One is Barbara Reynolds, a prominent black journalist, author, and ordained minister who would like to back the movement because of what it represents. But she is uncomfortable with and sometimes appalled by the actions of many of its activists. "The baby boomers who drove the success of the civil rights movement want to get behind Black Lives Matter, but the group's confrontational and divisive tactics make it difficult," says Reynolds. She is deeply troubled by the actions of many

Riot police stand ready to act after angry mobs began burning buildings and police cars in Ferguson, Missouri. The riots followed a grand jury decision to not indict police officer Darren Wilson in the killing of Michael Brown three months earlier.

people at Black Lives Matter demonstrations, as she writes: "It is difficult to distinguish legitimate activists from the mob actors who burn and loot. The demonstrations are peppered with hate speech, profanity, and guys with sagging pants that show their underwear. Even if the [Black Lives Matter] activists aren't the ones participating in the boorish language and dress, neither are they condemning it."[47]

With her mention of burning and looting, Reynolds is referring to violent protests such as the one in Ferguson, Missouri, after Darren Wilson shot and killed Michael Brown. In November 2014, when a grand jury announced that there was insufficient evidence to indict Wilson for a crime, pandemonium broke out in Ferguson. Brown's stepfather angrily said, "Burn this bitch down!"[48]—and a large, angry crowd took him literally. Buildings throughout the city were burned, and several police cars were set on fire. Angry mobs broke the windows of businesses and looted them, stealing from restaurants, mobile phone stores, grocery stores, liquor stores, and pharmacies, among others. Protesters charged police barricades and hurled glass bottles. Law enforcement responded by firing smoke canisters, teargas grenades, and sting grenades, which eject dozens of rubber bullets and powdered chemicals into the area surrounding the device.

> "The baby boomers who drove the success of the civil rights movement want to get behind Black Lives Matter, but the group's confrontational and divisive tactics make it difficult."[47]
>
> —Barbara Reynolds, a journalist and minister who was part of the 1960s civil rights movement

Reynolds does credit Black Lives Matter for how it embraces black women as leaders. "In this way," she says, "[Black Lives Matter] has improved on the previous generation," which she calls "sexist to the core." But she would like to see more efforts made to be inclusive rather than divisive, as the movement tends to be. "To win broader appeal," says Reynolds, "it must work harder to acknowledge humanity in the lives of others. The movement loses sympathy when it shouts down those who dare to utter 'all lives matter.' . . . The civil rights movement was not exclusively a black movement for black people. It valued all human lives, even those who worked against us."[49]

What the Public Thinks

Many people who oppose Black Lives Matter claim that the movement has caused racial relations to deteriorate. This was the consensus of a July 2016 CBS News/*New York Times* poll that questioned sixteen hundred adults. Only 26 percent thought race relations in the United States are mostly good, which was a drop of 11 points from the year before. In fact, the 26 percent was a low not seen since the 1992 race riots in Los Angeles, California.

Another poll in July 2016 also addressed race issues. Conducted by Monmouth University in New Jersey, the poll revealed that more Americans see racial discrimination as a major problem than did so in 2015. A majority of participants (58 percent) felt that Black Lives Matter has brought attention to racial inequality in American society. Many white respondents said the movement had made racial issues worse, and only 10 percent of total participants thought Black Lives Matter had made racial issues better. "Most Americans agree that Black Lives Matter has shined a light on important issues of race," says Patrick Murray,

Blue Lives Matter Laws

High-profile police killings such as the shooting deaths of two New York City officers in December 2014 and the 2016 killing of five police officers in Dallas, Texas, have led to calls for new laws to protect police. As of March 2017, fourteen US states had introduced Blue Lives Matter legislation. These laws aimed to provide police officers the same protections from hate crimes as have been granted to ethnic and religious minorities and lesbian, gay, bisexual, and transgender (LGBT) citizens. Louisiana was the first state to introduce such legislation; it was signed into law by the governor in May 2016. Similar legislation in other states has not fared well, with most of the bills voted down, referred to committees, or left to expire when legislative sessions ended.

Opponents of such legislation argue that the penalties for killing a police officer are already harsh. People who commit such acts, for instance, usually receive the death penalty. Also, opponents point out, despite a spike in police killings during 2016, violence against police officers has steadily declined over the years, making such legislation unnecessary. Criminologist Jack Levin explains, "This [recent spike in police killings] is, hopefully, a short-term blip and not a trend. If we see that the number of ambushes of police officers continues to rise, then it may be worth taking another look at the possibility of including them in hate crime laws."

Quoted in Julia Craven, "32 Blue Lives Matter Bills Have Been Introduced Across 14 States This Year," *Huffington Post*, March 1, 2017. www.huffingtonpost.com.

director of the Monmouth University Polling Institute, "but there is a significant split on the impact that attention is having."[50]

No Simple Answers

Opinions about Black Lives Matter are plentiful and as diverse as the thousands of people who are part of it. Many people blame the movement for anti–law enforcement sentiment and even hold activists responsible for police killings. Others counter that the movement should not be held responsible, because such violence is not what it stands for. Older civil rights activists frown on the tactics used by today's activists and are hesitant to support the movement. This backlash has caused serious challenges for those who support Black Lives Matter and has likely contributed to public opinion that race relations are worse because of the movement. Whether these rifts can be resolved will depend on whether people on both sides are willing to listen and try to understand each other's point of view.

CHAPTER FOUR

Law Enforcement Accountability

On Saturday, April 29, 2017, a black high school freshman named Jordan Edwards was shot to death by Roy Durwood Oliver, a white police officer. Edwards, a straight-A student and standout athlete, had attended a house party in Balch Springs, Texas, with his two brothers and a couple of friends. The party had gotten large and rowdy, so the teens decided to leave. They were in a car backing out of a parking space when Oliver yelled at them to stop. He and another officer had gone to the home after a 911 caller complained about a wild party and drunk teenagers. When the car Edwards was riding in did not stop as Oliver had ordered, he grabbed a rifle from his police cruiser and opened fire. The barrage of gunshots shattered the front passenger-side window and struck Edwards in the back of the head. The teen was taken to a hospital, where he was pronounced dead.

Initially, Oliver claimed that he fired on the car because the driver was backing up, fast and aggressively, toward the officers—but body camera footage told a different story. In May 2017, Oliver was fired from his job, arrested, and charged with murder. "We want this to stop happening," says Lee Merritt, an attorney for the Edwards family. "Every other modern nation in the world has figured out how to police their citizens without killing so many of them. . . . We demand justice for #JordanEdwards. We demand a change."[51]

A Fine Line
When police officers are dispatched to the scene of a crime, or even just an unruly house party, they never know what to expect.

This uncertainty is one aspect of the job that can be stressful for those in law enforcement. When encountering a situation they find threatening, police may have to use force—even kill, if necessary. But as hard as it may be, they must also use sound judgment and keep a cool head in chaotic situations. The only lawful reason for police officers to use a firearm is in the case of a direct threat, either to their lives or the lives of others. Most police officers follow this mandate in the course of performing their jobs, as the US Department of Justice (DOJ) explains: "The vast majority of the law enforcement officers in the country perform their very difficult jobs with respect for their communities and in compliance with the law."[52] Yet in some cases, as shown by Oliver's decision to shoot at a carload of teenagers, it is clear that sound judgment did not prevail.

Even though police officers are authority figures who are sworn to uphold the law, this does not mean they are *above* the law. Those who abuse their authority or use excessive force can be charged with a crime. If they have infringed on someone's constitutional rights, the federal government (through the DOJ) may become involved. NPR law enforcement correspondent Martin Kaste says when the "feds" bring charges, "it's if they see evidence of a constitutional violation, a willful deprivation of someone's civil rights."[53]

Aside from constitutional rights, which police officers are sworn to uphold, laws and rules about police comportment and use of force often differ from state to state and from city to city. In Minneapolis, Minnesota, for instance, a police officer was arrested in March 2017 and charged with third-degree felony assault for brutally kicking a thirty-five-year-old suspect. The kicking assault was considered excessive use of force, as the officer repeatedly kicked the man in the face, which caused a traumatic brain injury. The officer's fate might have been different in another state.

Many police departments have rules about takedown maneuvers used on suspects. Officers with the New York City Police Department (NYPD), for example, are forbidden to use a tech-

> "The vast majority of the law enforcement officers in the country perform their very difficult jobs with respect for their communities and in compliance with the law."[52]
>
> —The DOJ, the United States' top law enforcement agency

A police officer subdues a protester during a demonstration. Police officers sometimes must use force, but they must also show good judgment and be able to stay calm during extremely stressful situations.

nique known as the choke hold (sometimes called a stranglehold). Choke holds involve bending an arm around someone's neck to get a tight hold, which subdues the person by restricting his or her breathing. In 1993, when the NYPD announced its ban on the maneuver, it referred to choke holds as "potentially lethal and unnecessary."[54] The NYPD granted exceptions only when an officer's life was in danger and a choke hold was absolutely necessary and the only possible way to subdue a suspect.

The Deadly Choke Hold

In July 2014 a police officer from Staten Island, New York, named Daniel Pantaleo broke the NYPD's rule about choke holds—and in doing so, he killed someone. Pantaleo and another plainclothes officer approached Eric Garner, a forty-three-year-old African American man, on suspicion that he was illegally selling untaxed loose cigarettes. He had been caught selling "loosies" on several occasions, so the police were familiar with him. Garner denied the charge and began arguing with the officers, asking why they always harassed him. Pantaleo then moved to handcuff him, and Garner put his arms up and backed away, saying not to touch him. Pantaleo grabbed Garner in a choke hold and began squeezing his neck, and then pushed him to the pavement and rolled him over onto his stomach. Garner, who was obese and suffered from asthma and heart disease, began gasping and pleading, "I can't breathe."[55] According to a cell phone video that was shot by his friend, Ramsey Orta, Garner repeated that he could not breathe eleven times. And then he lost consciousness.

Gwen Garner, mother of Eric Garner who died after being subjected to a police choke hold, speaks at a rally in 2017. After her son's 2014 death and the grand jury's decision to not indict the officer, Gwen Garner expressed extreme disappointment with the justice system.

The officers delayed in calling an ambulance, and for unknown reasons, when paramedics arrived they did not give Garner oxygen. Finally, he was transported to the hospital, where he was pronounced dead. The medical examiner who performed an autopsy ruled that Garner's death was a homicide. Pantaleo was put on desk duty rather than active patrol while the case was reviewed to see whether criminal charges were warranted. In December 2014 a grand jury announced that Pantaleo would not be indicted for Garner's death.

People throughout the United States had seen the video of Garner repeatedly saying he could not breathe. When the public learned that Pantaleo would walk away from Garner's killing without being held accountable, many were outraged. In a public statement after the grand jury's announcement, Garner's mother said: "I am truly disappointed in the grand jury's decision this evening. . . . How could we put our trust in the justice system when they fail us like this?"[56] Soon, the phrase "I can't breathe" started appearing on signs and banners displayed at Black Lives Matter demonstrations. Kobe Bryant and other professional athletes wore shirts saying "I can't breathe" in silent protest. "I can't breathe" became a rallying cry for the oppression of black citizens by police officers.

The Blue Code of Silence

Even though Pantaleo had clearly caused Garner's death and had a number of prior complaints for using excessive force on suspects, the NYPD still stood by him. He was not fired after the autopsy results were announced or when the video became public. Police officer and police union president Patrick Lynch called Pantaleo a "model of what we want a police officer to be,"[57] saying he was mature and motivated by serving his community. This strong sense of loyalty is common among police officers, who typically cover for each other and defend one another no matter what the circumstances are. This is known as the blue code (or blue wall) of silence, an unwritten rule that is rarely broken. Those who violate it and speak out against a fellow officer risk retaliation by other police officers.

Author and political analyst Earl Ofari Hutchinson refers to the blue code of silence as a "deep, prevalent, and terrifying" aspect

Exposing Police Brutality

On April 4, 2015, Feidin Santana was walking to work at a barber shop in North Charleston, South Carolina, when he noticed a white police officer struggling with a black man. The officer, Michael Slager, had Walter Scott on the ground and seemed to be in control of the situation. Then Scott jumped up and started running away, and Santana instinctively hit the record button on his cell phone. He was recording as Slager opened fire on Scott, shooting him in the back a total of eight times. Santana was horrified at what he had seen, and out of fear of what might happen to him, he tried to forget about the video. At one point, he considered erasing it from his phone. Then he read the police report and saw that Slager had lied about what happened. He claimed that Scott took his stun gun and tried to use it against him, and he shot the man out of fear for his life. Santana knew that was not the truth, as he had seen the whole thing. "I got mad," he says.

Santana took the video to Scott's family, and they released it to the media. Slager was charged with murder. After a mistrial, he pleaded guilty to a lesser charge and as of May 2017 was awaiting sentencing—a maximum of life in prison. For exposing what had been done to Scott, Santana was honored by the civil rights group Los Angeles Urban Policy Roundtable, which presented him with its Civic Engagement Award.

Quoted in James Quelly and David Zucchino, "Man Who Recorded Walter Scott Shooting Says His Life Has Changed Forever," *Los Angeles Times*, April 9, 2015. www.latimes.com.

of police culture. He references a comprehensive National Institute of Ethics study in which hundreds of police officers in twenty-one states were surveyed. Nearly 80 percent of officers said that a code of silence exists, and more than half of those were not bothered by it. Nearly half of the officers surveyed admitted that the code was strongest when excessive force was used. Half of the officers also admitted they had witnessed misconduct by another officer but kept quiet about it. "Why?" Hutchinson asks. "Because in many cases they were told to keep quiet by other officers and in even more cases by department higher-ups."[58]

If officers did not keep the offense to themselves, says Hutchinson, they could be shunned by their peers, be held responsible for another officer's firing, and/or lose their own jobs. "At the very least [they] would be 'blackballed,' or . . . their bosses would simply blow their complaint off. A significant number of them said they wanted to speak out about the abusive acts of fellow officers but were pressured by "uninvolved officers" to keep quiet.[59]

An Unjustified Shooting

In being bound by the blue code of silence, it is not uncommon for police officers to lie in order to protect each other. One highly publicized example of this occurred after the death of seventeen-year-old Laquan McDonald from Chicago, Illinois. On the evening of October 20, 2014, Chicago police were called to investigate a black male (McDonald) who was armed with a knife and breaking into vehicles in a trucking yard. When police confronted McDonald, he slashed the tires on one of the patrol cars and refused to drop the knife when ordered to do so. Officer Jason Van Dyke opened fire on McDonald, and after the teen fell to the payment and lay there, Van Dyke continued shooting him. The teen was transported to a hospital, where he was pronounced dead. An autopsy report stated that Van Dyke had shot McDonald a total of sixteen times—in the chest, back, neck, scalp, arms, and right hand and leg.

> "This is the classic code of silence situation where you have an incident go down and you've got multiple police officers who all feel obligated to help cover the behavior of police officers."[60]
>
> —Terry Ekl, a criminal defense attorney

Initially, Van Dyke claimed that he fired his gun only after McDonald lunged at him with the knife and refused to drop it. Six other police officers who were on the scene lied to protect Van Dyke. They backed his account of what happened when he contended that McDonald was waving the knife around and fully intended to injure or kill Van Dyke, who then had no choice but to defend himself. Says Terry Ekl, a criminal defense attorney:

> This is the classic code of silence situation where you have an incident go down and you've got multiple police officers who all feel obligated to help cover the behavior of police officers. Those examples happen over and over and over again. . . . Before you know it, an entire community of people do not trust the police, they do not respect the police, they do not like the police. And that is the situation we have now.[60]

The police officers who lied to protect Van Dyke were caught. The shooting was recorded by cameras mounted on the patrol car dashboards (known as dash cams). The Chicago Police Department tried to keep the video footage a secret and did not release it until ordered to do so by a state judge thirteen months later. Van Dyke was criminally charged for McDonald's death. A grand jury later indicted him on six counts of first-degree murder and sixteen counts of aggravated battery—one for each time he shot McDonald. In August 2016 Chicago police superintendent Eddie Johnson announced that all the officers who had lied on Van Dyke's behalf were being fired from their jobs. As of May 2017 Van Dyke's trial was still pending.

Rare Convictions

Van Dyke's murder charge was a rarity in the history of the Chicago Police Department. He was the first Chicago police officer in nearly thirty-five years to be charged with murder for an on-duty shooting. Since 2007 an independent Chicago review authority has investigated nearly four hundred police shootings in the city, and all but one were deemed justified. Critics claim that the review authority itself is biased toward the police, and cite the improbability that only one of four hundred shootings was unjustified. And the low number of Chicago convictions is consistent with national figures. According to a 2016 *Washington Post* investigation, the prosecution of police officers is extremely rare, with charges filed in only about 1 percent of all fatal police shootings. And even if police officers are charged and indicted with a crime, juries are often reluctant to convict them.

This trend may be starting to change, however. Another finding of the *Washington Post* investigation was that indictments of police officers have tripled in the past decade. During 2016, for instance, thirteen officers were charged, and during the prior year eighteen were charged. This is in stark contrast to the years 2005 to 2014, when only about five officers per year were charged. The upturn is largely due to the increased use of technology, such as video cameras used by bystanders, body cameras worn by police, and dash cam technology.

One of the few police officers who was indicted and convicted in a shooting death was Stephen Rankin, from Portsmouth, Virginia.

A Miami, Florida police officer demonstrates the use of a body camera. Increased use of technology, including body cameras, might explain the higher numbers of indictments against police officers in the last couple years.

In April 2015 Rankin responded to a shoplifting call at a Walmart store. Upon arrival in the parking lot, Rankin confronted the suspect, eighteen-year-old William Chapman II. When Rankin was unable to get handcuffs on the teen, there was a struggle and Rankin began shooting. Chapman, who was unarmed, died at the scene, and an autopsy found that he had been shot eleven times. In August 2016 a jury found Rankin guilty of voluntary manslaughter. Even though prosecutors had recommended that he serve ten years in prison, the jury's recommendation was only two and a half years.

After the verdict was announced, Chapman's mother was bereft and emotional, saying that such a short sentence was nowhere near enough punishment for what had been done to her son. But other Chapman supporters were encouraged by the

Body Cams

When a police officer has killed someone, it can be challenging, or even impossible, to prove whether the killing was justified. This became a source of widespread outrage in 2014 when Officer Darren Wilson shot Michael Brown to death in Ferguson, Missouri. The scenario as told by Brown's friend and other witnesses was very different from Wilson's own account of what happened, and a grand jury opted not to indict the officer, based on insufficient evidence. If he had been wearing a body camera, or body cam, the outcome might have been different, although there is no way to know that for sure.

Body cams are small, specialized video recorders that attach to the front of a police officer's uniform. Some of these gadgets are tiny enough to clip onto a collar, a hat, or the frame of glasses or sunglasses. As police officers generate recordings throughout the course of their time on duty, videos are stored in the devices. The video files can then be uploaded to a department server or to external cloud storage. Should questions arise about an officer's actions, the footage can be reviewed and, if warranted, used as evidence at a trial. "It's the best available evidence that's neutral," says Steve Tuttle, who is with the camera manufacturer TASER. "It's just an observer. The truth is the truth."

Quoted in Shirley Li, "The Big Picture: How Do Police Body Cams Work?," *Atlantic*, August 25, 2014. www.the atlantic.com.

verdict, viewing it as a turning point for people of color and the Black Lives Matter movement. "We had to start somewhere," says Chapman's cousin Earl Lewis. "This was the beginning."[61]

What Cops Say

Even though police officers abide by the blue code of silence, when they are anonymously surveyed, they acknowledge that bad cops are not often held accountable. This was revealed during a January 2017 Pew Research Center survey, which involved nearly eight thousand law enforcement officers throughout the United States. The survey also highlighted the tensions between law enforcement and many of the communities they serve. Also evident from their feedback was the difference in perspectives among black and white officers. For instance, 69 percent of black officers believe that Black Lives Matter activists are at least somewhat motivated by a legitimate interest in increasing police accountability. Of the white officers surveyed, only 27 percent shared that belief. An even more stark contrast was in perspectives about whether the country has already made the needed changes to achieve racial equality. Among white officers, 92 percent agreed with the statement, compared with just 8 percent of black officers.

Although black and white officers may disagree about issues concerning race and policing, most agree that police are not always viewed fairly. Journalist Daniel Knowles spent time interviewing police officers to learn their perspectives on the debate over policing in the United States. One common perspective the officers shared with him was that the media vilify the police and make them look as if they are all bad guys when that is not true. As one police lieutenant from a midwestern community told Knowles, "It sometimes feels like the only voice you ever hear is criticizing you. . . . If you watch the TV news, our good work only gets two seconds. When we do something bad, it gets two minutes."[62]

> "It sometimes feels like the only voice you ever hear is criticizing you. . . . If you watch the TV news, our good work only gets two seconds. When we do something bad, it gets two minutes."[62]
>
> —A police lieutenant from a midwestern community

Tough Choices

Police officers have an important job to do, and society depends on them to help keep people and communities safe. A cop's job can be tough, stressful, and also dangerous, and he or she must be prepared to deal with any situation. If officers are faced with a threat, it may be necessary for them to defend themselves or someone else, possibly by taking another's life. That is considered an unfortunate part of a police officer's job. And when sound judgment and good sense fail and excessive force is used, it is the police department's and community's job to hold offending officers accountable.

CHAPTER FIVE

Improving Policing, Strengthening Relationships

In August 2014, when Ferguson, Missouri, erupted into a storm of protest over Michael Brown's shooting by a white police officer, Bruce Franks Jr. was in the midst of it all. A native of St. Louis and a rapper who goes by the stage name of Ooops, Franks drove to Ferguson after the shooting happened. At first he had no clear reason to be there, since he was not really into activism. But after a few nights of breathing teargas as police fired it into crowds, Franks was fed up and screaming for justice. "THERE IS A WAR BEING WAGED UPON US," he wrote on his Facebook page. "IF THERE IS NO JUSTICE, I WILL SHOW YOU EXACTLY WHAT NO PEACE LOOKS LIKE."[63]

While in Ferguson, Franks met a peace activist named Paul Muhammad, the founder of an informal group called Ferguson Peacekeepers. Muhammad's first impression of Franks was that he was a hotheaded protester who wanted to tear things apart. But Franks's impression of Muhammad was nothing like that. He admired Muhammad's work with the group of people who acted as a "buffer of love" between police and protesters so the latter could safely speak out. Franks asked if he could join the group, and Muhammad said he could—as long as Franks adhered to certain standards. "If you're gonna put on this [Peacekeepers] hoodie, you have to be a de-escalator and watch out for agitators," said Muhammad. "We're with the movement, but if they're throwing rocks and bottles, you need to step to [confront] those people."[64] Franks agreed and joined the group. That was the start of a renewed focus for him, and he went on to become a well-known—and well-connected—antiviolence activist.

An Unlikely Police Ally

In March 2015 Franks founded his own grassroots organization called 28 to Life. Its name came from the (now debunked) statistic that a black person is killed by a cop every twenty-eight hours. Franks's mission was simple: to save black lives. He realized that in order to do that, he had to build relationships with people in law enforcement, and that is what he set out to do.

Once an unapologetic basher of police officers, Franks is now on friendly terms with a number of them. He gets text messages from the St. Louis police chief. He gets tweeted by city circuit attorney Jennifer Joyce, whom he refers to as J.J. He acts as a

Violence erupted in August 2014 during a protest over the police shooting death of an unarmed black teenager in Ferguson, Missouri. Protests—some peaceful, some violent—shook the nation.

consultant to the city, including the St. Louis Police Department, and meets often with Joyce as well as police chiefs, police academy candidates, and St. Louis City Hall leaders, among others. The guy who once had only negative thoughts about police officers is now influencing public safety policy at the highest levels. "I got to know him and realized right away that when this person calls, I need to answer the phone," says Jon Belmar, St. Louis County police chief. "He has no problem telling you when you've messed up, but he has the ability to listen and work things out. He's invested in this, and for the right reasons. I can't tell you how valuable that is."[65]

> "When we think about what Eric Garner was doing the day that he was killed after being choked on Staten Island—selling loose cigarettes should never be something that lands you in a coffin."[67]
>
> —Black Lives Matter activist and leader Brittany Packnett

One challenge Franks faces (although he does not let it get in his way) is hostility on the part of activists in his native St. Louis—people who still hate police just as he once did. He has been called a traitor and a spy by those who have no respect for anyone who works with law enforcement. "I get why people are skeptical," says Black Lives Matter's DeRay Mckesson. But Mckesson also understands why Franks does what he does, and he admires Franks for taking an active role in trying to bring about improved police-community relationships. "He doesn't play a role that I would play," says Mckesson. "But he has clear reasons as to why he engages this way, and he has integrity."[66]

Campaign Zero

Although Mckesson's approach is different from that of Franks, he is also involved in trying to change the way police interact with black citizens. Together with fellow Black Lives Matter activists Johnetta Elzie, Brittany Packnett, and Sam Sinyangwe, Mckesson launched an endeavor called Campaign Zero. It is a police reform effort that calls for stronger guidelines that limit the use of force by police officers. One of the group's goals is to end a police practice known as "broken windows." The approach is based on the theory that by ridding a community of low-level crimes

People Helping Police

With the ongoing battles between civil rights activists and police in the United States, it can seem like everyone is against law enforcement. But during protests in Baltimore, Maryland, in 2015, a group of citizens took action to help protect police from demonstrators. The protests erupted after the death of twenty-five-year-old Freddie Gray. Gray had been arrested by Baltimore police for alleged illegal possession of a switchblade. During the arrest, officers put Gray into a tactical hold. Restrained with handcuffs and leg irons, he was loaded into a police van headfirst, on his stomach. While being transported in the van, Gray was not secured with a seat belt, which was in violation of Baltimore Police Department policy. He fell into a coma during the ride and was taken to a trauma center, where he was diagnosed with severe injuries to his spinal cord. Gray died at the trauma center a week later.

When people in Baltimore learned what had happened to Gray, the city erupted into violence. Streets became war zones, as police cars were burned, looters robbed stores and businesses, and rioters pummeled police with rocks, bricks, bottles, and even cinder blocks. Six police officers were seriously injured. Finally, a group of black men decided enough was enough. They joined hands and formed a human barrier between police officers and protesters. They said they were not with any particular group. They were just there to "protect law enforcement, as well as other citizens—to be an extra layer."

Quoted in Carla Herreria, "Iconic Baltimore Photo Resurfaces, Spreading Healing Message We All Need," *Huffington Post*, July 13, 2016. www.huffingtonpost.com.

(such as trespassing or disorderly conduct), it becomes a better, more desirable place for people to live, one where subsequent and more serious crimes are less likely to occur.

The problem with this thinking, says Packnett, is that tough enforcement of low-level crimes often affects black people far more than it does whites. It has also resulted in a number of preventable deaths. Packnett explains:

> When we think about what Eric Garner was doing the day that he was killed after being choked on Staten Island—selling loose cigarettes should never be something that

lands you in a coffin. And so when we think about the criminalization of blackness of marginalized communities, it often begins with the enforcement of these very low-level crimes with overzealous and overuse of force.[67]

A recent focus of Campaign Zero is fighting what its founders believe is a serious threat to black communities by the Trump administration. In January 2017, just before Donald Trump was inaugurated, Campaign Zero linked to a website called the Trump Resistance Manual. The website covers proposed policies on health care, immigration, and mass incarceration. Visitors to the site are encouraged to get involved in local activism on behalf of police reform issues, as well as LGBT rights, education, and climate change, among others. Yet even as Campaign Zero expands into a variety of issues, police reform remains its highest priority.

Members of Campaign Zero believe that President Donald Trump's policies represent a threat to black communities across the United States. Although their priority is still police reform, the group has begun working on other causes.

Building Trust Between Police and Communities

Just as activists are working to improve relationships between the police and the black communities they serve, so too are police departments. Because of serious breakdowns in those relationships, and the violence that has resulted from those breakdowns, many police departments throughout the United States are taking steps to address the problem. This was the focus of an event called the Bridge Summit that was held in Phoenix, Arizona, in September 2015. Six police chiefs (five of whom were African American) from major US cities shared their stories about what has worked in their communities. In addition to Phoenix, the police chiefs were from Cleveland, Ohio; Denver, Colorado; Atlanta, Georgia; Seattle, Washington; and Oakland, California.

Of all the ways to build relationships between citizens and police, the chiefs agreed that striving to have a racially diverse police force is a high priority. "With a disproportionately White, male force," says journalist Kim Covington, who attended the summit, "police are doubling recruitment efforts" to fill open police department positions "with more racial and cultural minorities as well as women."[68] Police chiefs also talked about other practices that have proved to be effective in their communities. In Denver, for instance, police officers are trained to rethink whether enforcement of a law is really necessary before issuing a ticket. Maybe deciding not to issue a parking ticket, for instance, could help improve relationships with citizens who assume police are going to harass and/or arrest them.

The police chief from Atlanta spoke about a unique program in his city. The police foundation raises money to give officers a financial incentive to live in refurbished homes in the city at no cost for two years. The thinking is that the more police officers who live in the neighborhoods they serve and protect, the better their community relationships will be. And in Oakland, police officers receive stress and fear training. This training can help officers react more appropriately in stressful circumstances and help de-escalate potentially volatile situations.

Notably, says Covington, not one of the strategies or programs shared by the police chiefs involved weapons. "It was refreshing," she says, "to hear that at least these leaders are focusing on the heart and the head of a police officer."[69]

Improved Policing Policies

The ideas shared by the Bridge Summit police chiefs represent the kind of thinking that could help build better community relationships. Police departments in many American cities are implementing new policies and programs based on such thinking. In August 2016, Minneapolis, Minnesota, Police Chief Janeé Harteau announced some major changes in her department. One addition will be de-escalation training for police officers. Before resorting to force, officers will be trained to exhaust all reasonable means of defusing potentially violent situations. This is one of many initiatives put in place by Harteau that are aimed at restoring citizens' trust in law enforcement. "We cannot have public safety without public trust,"[70] she says.

Another addition to police officer training in Minneapolis is learning to recognize factors that might contribute to someone's lack of compliance. These could include language barriers, drug and alcohol use, or a mental health crisis.

> "We cannot have public safety without public trust."[70]
>
> —Janeé Harteau, police chief of Minneapolis, Minnesota

And in situations where force becomes necessary, officers are encouraged to first announce their intent to use force. Also, says Harteau, the Minneapolis Police Department has outfitted all officers with body cameras. In cases where excessive force is used, video footage can help ensure the offending officer is dealt with appropriately. And because policing can be stressful and tough on officers emotionally, the Minneapolis Police Department overhauled its early intervention system. This will allow the department to better identify potentially troubled officers and help them get the care they need.

Dallas: A Police Reform Success Story

A number of policy changes have also been implemented in Dallas, Texas. Led by Police Chief David O. Brown, the force has become known as a model of community policing. This has not always been the case in the city, as journalist Christopher I. Haugh explains: "Dallas was once notorious for police violence. For years, the third largest city in Texas has had a higher per-capita rate of police-involved shootings than Chicago, New York, or Los Angeles."[71]

A Minneapolis police officer talks with two young Minnesotans as part of a community policing effort in neighborhoods that are home to people of color. Efforts like this one are being instituted in many US cities.

To change that disturbing trend and build a police force that citizens could trust, Brown enacted a number of community policing measures. One was a new foot pursuit policy that emphasizes de-escalation. Officers are trained to think carefully about a situation before reacting and to back off if that is the smartest choice. Brown is also committed to transparency, meaning that police statistics—including data on shootings—will not be kept from the public; they are now accessible online. In talking to his officers, Brown also declared that traffic tickets were not intended to raise revenue. As a result, the number of tickets issued by officers was slashed in half. In addition, just as in Minneapolis, more officers on the Dallas force were issued body cameras.

As a result of these and other measures in the Dallas police department, excessive-force complaints against officers declined by 64 percent over a five-year period. In a July 9, 2016, article, Brown stated: "So far this year, in 2016, we have had four excessive force complaints. We've averaged between 150 and 200 my whole career. So this is transformative." He also noted a decrease in the number of police shootings. "We've averaged between 18 and 25 police involved shootings my whole career," Brown said. "We've had two so far this year."[72]

> "So far this year, in 2016, we have had four excessive force complaints. We've averaged between 150 and 200 my whole career. So this is transformative."[72]
>
> —Dallas police chief David O. Brown

Although Brown was devastated by the murder of five Dallas police officers during a Black Lives Matter protest, he remains hopeful that efforts to build community relationships will lessen the risk of violence in the city. One of his primary goals is to recruit more minorities to work as police officers. After the July 2016 shootings, Brown was emotional and distraught. At one point during a news conference, he directed his words to young black males who had been protesting police killings. "Become a part of the solution," Brown said. "We're hiring. Get off that protest line and put an application in. And we'll put you in your neighborhood, and we'll help you resolve some of the problems you're protesting about."[73]

High-Tech Law Enforcement

Whenever police chiefs talk about building community trust and cutting down on excessive force, they often mention the important role of technology. Although dash cams and body cams alone cannot solve all problems, they can help ensure that the truth comes out whenever police find it necessary to use force. In 2016 the Major Cities Chiefs Association and Major Counties Sheriffs' Association surveyed seventy law enforcement agencies throughout the United States. The purpose of the survey was to find out whether police departments were using body cams. Nearly all (95 percent) of the police chiefs surveyed were either committed to body cams or were already using the devices. Most of the 5 percent who were not in favor of body cams cited privacy concerns or fears that the video footage could be posted publicly online. But according to criminal justice expert David Roberts, these body cam opponents are not likely to hold out much longer. "Ultimately, they're going to need to adopt it," says Roberts. "Juries, prosecutors and the courts will demand it."[74]

By providing video evidence of officers' actions, body and dash cams provide reassurance to the community that officers will be held accountable for their actions. The presence of such cameras is also thought to influence police behavior, leading to fewer incidences of police misconduct. In addition, captured video can

Efforts to Achieve Diversity

Milwaukee, Wisconsin, is a city where 64 percent of the population is nonwhite. Law enforcement officials in Milwaukee understand the importance of a police force that reflects its citizens. "Clearly, we have to be reflective of all the communities we serve," says Milwaukee police chief Edward Flynn. "That's part of achieving trust and legitimacy." Yet only 34 percent of Milwaukee's officers and command staff are minorities, and this figure has not changed since 2008. According to an analysis by the *Milwaukee Journal-Sentinel*, black officers account for just 18 percent of the Milwaukee police force, and Hispanics account for 13 percent. Police academies have recruited a diverse pool of people, but many of them have dropped out.

To attract and retain qualified minorities, the Milwaukee Police Department has enacted measures that will hopefully make a positive difference. The department developed a ride-share program to help recruits get to work. To help them stay focused, the department sends out text and e-mail reminders. Also implemented was a mentoring program that involves practice test sessions to help recruits pass the tests necessary to become police officers. "I think so many of [these recruits] don't have supporters saying I'll drive you to the test, set the alarm clock, ask what time is that appointment?" says Flynn. "Even somebody in their early 20s still doesn't have their act entirely together."

Quoted in Ashley Luthern and Kevin Crowe, "Milwaukee Police Department Struggles to Increase Diversity in the Ranks," *Milwaukee Journal-Sentinel*, April 1, 2017. www.jsonline.com.

be used as a training tool to improve officers' performance. Using the video, an officer's actions can be critiqued after the fact, resulting in suggestions for improving inappropriate behavior.

Progress and Peril

From community policing initiatives to improved policies to implementing the latest high-tech equipment, law enforcement agencies throughout the United States are making an effort to do a better job of serving their communities. And they are being aided by activists who, though once ardent critics of the police, now work hand in hand with them to improve relationships between police officers and their community. There is no doubt that this is a monumental task, as there is a large gap between those who fear and mistrust police and those who work as police officers. In time, it is hoped, these strategies will make a positive difference. That hope is the one thing people on all sides of this issue share.

SOURCE NOTES

Introduction: Fighting for Equality

1. Quoted in Elizabeth Day, "#BlackLivesMatter: The Birth of a New Civil Rights Movement," *Guardian* (Manchester), July 19, 2015. www.theguardian.com.

2. Quoted in Day, "#BlackLivesMatter."

3. Quoted in Jelani Cobb, "The Matter of Black Lives," *New Yorker*, March 14, 2016. www.newyorker.com.

4. Quoted in Collier Meyerson, "Meet the Women Founders of Black Lives Matter," *Glamour*, November 1, 2016. www.glamour.com.

5. Quoted in Day, "#BlackLivesMatter."

6. Quoted in Phil Helsel, "Obama: All Americans Should Be Concerned About Police Shootings," NBC News, July 7, 2016. www.nbcnews.com.

7. Quoted in Meyerson, "Meet the Women Founders of Black Lives Matter."

Chapter One: The Dangerous Divide Between Black Citizens and Police

8. Nikole Hannah-Jones, "A Letter from Black America," *Politico*, March/April 2015. www.politico.com.

9. Hannah-Jones, "A Letter from Black America."

10. Hannah-Jones, "A Letter from Black America."

11. American Civil Liberties Union, "Racial Profiling," 2017. www.aclu.org.

12. American Civil Liberties Union, "Racial Profiling."

13. Caleb Roberts, "Racial Profiling Raises Its Ugly Head (Again): A Night in the Life of a Black Man in Milwaukee," *Speak Freely* (blog), American Civil Liberties Union, February 22, 2017. www.aclu.org.

14. Roberts, "Racial Profiling Raises Its Ugly Head (Again)."

15. US Department of Justice, "Investigation of the Ferguson Police Department," March 4, 2015. www.justice.gov.

16. Quoted in Rachel Clarke and Christopher Lett, "What Happened When Michael Brown Met Officer Darren Wilson," CNN, November 11, 2014. www.cnn.com.

17. Quoted in Julie Bosman and Joseph Goldstein, "Timeline for a Body: 4 Hours in the Middle of a Ferguson Street," *New York Times*, August 23, 2014. https://mobile.nytimes.com.

18. James E. Causey, "Why African-Americans Don't Trust the Cops," *Milwaukee Journal-Sentinel*, April 8, 2015. http://archive.jsonline.com.

19. Causey, "Why African-Americans Don't Trust the Cops."

Chapter Two: The Formation of a Movement

20. Tef Poe, "Creating," Twitter, August 9, 2014. https://twitter.com.

21. Cobb, "The Matter of Black Lives."

22. Keith Lawrence and Terry Keleher, "Structural Racism," Race and Public Policy Conference, 2004. www.intergroupresources.com.

23. Quoted in Sarah Mervosh, "A Black Dallas Family 'Did Everything America Said We Should' but Still Endures Racism Daily," *Dallas News*, February 5, 2017. www.dallasnews.com.

24. Josh Hafner, "How Michael Brown's Death, Two Years Ago, Pushed #BlackLivesMatter into a Movement," *USA Today*, August 10, 2016. www.usatoday.com.

25. Quoted in *People*, "Oprah Winfrey's Comments About Recent Protests and Ferguson Spark Controversy," January 1, 2015. http://people.com.

26. Quoted in Aaron Randle, "Now You See Me: A Look at the World of Activist Johnetta Elzie," *Complex*, March 8, 2016. www.complex.com.

27. Quoted in Shannon Luibrand, "How a Death in Ferguson Sparked a Movement in America," CBS News, August 7, 2015. www.cbsnews.com.

28. Quoted in Day, "#BlackLivesMatter."

29. Quoted in Luibrand, "How a Death in Ferguson Sparked a Movement in America."

30. Quoted in Kristina Monllos, "How DeRay Mckesson Turned Social Media into a Powerful Tool for Social Justice," *Adweek*, October 30, 2016. www.adweek.com.

31. Sara Sidner and Mallory Simon, "The Rise of Black Lives Matter: Trying to Break the Cycle of Violence and Silence," CNN, December 28, 2015. www.cnn.com.

32. Deen Freelon et al., *Beyond the Hashtags*. Washington, DC: Center for Media & Social Impact, 2016. http://cmsimpact.org.

33. Quoted in Sidner and Simon, "The Rise of Black Lives Matter."

34. Quoted in *Code Switch*, "Jelani Cobb on His Epic 'New Yorker' Piece on Black Lives Matter," NPR, March 9, 2016. www.npr.org.

35. Quoted in Cobb, "The Matter of Black Lives."

Chapter Three: The Backlash

36. Quoted in Tessa Berenson, "Reverend Who Organized Dallas Protest: 'It Was All About Love,'" *Time*, July 8, 2016. http://time.com.

37. Quoted in Bill Chappell, "'We're Hurting,' Dallas Police Chief David Brown Says," NPR, July 8, 2016. www.npr.org.

38. Quoted in Jay Reeves and Errin Haines Whack, "Black Lives Matter Condemns Dallas Shootings, Plans Protests," *U.S. News & World Report*, July 8, 2016. www.usnews.com.

39. Black Lives Matter, "The Black Lives Matter Network Advocates for Dignity, Justice, and Respect," July 2016. http://blacklivesmatter.com.

40. Quoted in David Weigel, "Texas Republicans Blame Black Lives Matter for Shooting of Dallas Police," *Washington Post*, July 8, 2016. www.washingtonpost.com.

41. Quoted in Day, "#BlackLivesMatter."

42. Quoted in Doug Stanglin and Marco della Cava, "Suspect Named in Killing of Houston Deputy," *USA Today*, August 29, 2015. www.usatoday.com.

43. Blue Lives Matter, "About Us," 2017. https://bluelivesmatter .blue.

44. Natasha Lennard, "After Dallas, We Don't Need to Say 'Blue Lives Matter,'" *Rolling Stone*, July 8, 2016. www.rollingstone .com.

45. Quoted in *Seattle Times*, "Black Lives Matter Protest in Seattle Discourages Hate Toward Police: 'We Need You,'" July 22, 2016. www.seattletimes.com.

46. Peniel Joseph, "The Problem with Blaming Black Lives Matter," CNN, July 19, 2016. www.cnn.com.

47. Barbara Reynolds, "I Was a Civil Rights Activist in the 1960s. But It's Hard for Me to Get Behind Black Lives Matter," *Washington Post*, August 24, 2015. www.washingtonpost.com.

48. Quoted in Ray Sanchez, "Michael Brown's Stepfather at Rally: "Burn This Bitch Down!," CNN, November 25, 2014. www .cnn.com.

49. Reynolds, "I Was a Civil Rights Activist in the 1960s. But It's Hard for Me to Get Behind Black Lives Matter."

50. Quoted in Monmouth University, "Race Relations Worsen," July 19, 2016. www.monmouth.edu.

Chapter Four: Law Enforcement Accountability

51. Quoted in Tom Cleary, "Roy Oliver: 5 Fast Facts You Need to Know," Heavy, May 2, 2017. http://heavy.com.

52. US Department of Justice, "Addressing Police Misconduct," August 6, 2015. www.justice.gov.

53. Martin Kaste, "Alton Sterling Case Raises Questions About Prosecution of Police Officers," NPR, May 3, 2017. www.npr.org.

54. Quoted in Conor Friedersdorf, "Eric Garner and the NYPD's History of Deadly Chokeholds," *Atlantic*, December 4, 2014. www.theatlantic.com.

55. Quoted in Joseph Goldstein and Nate Schweber, "Man's Death After Chokehold Raises Old Issue for the Police," *New York Times*, July 19, 2014. www.nytimes.com.

56. Quoted in Lauren Barbato, "Esaw Garner, Eric Garner's Widow, Says 'This Fight Ain't Over,'" *Bustle*, December 3, 2014. www.bustle.com.

57. Quoted in Dugald McConnell and Brian Todd, "Defenders of Cop Involved in Garner Death Say He's a 'Model Officer,'" CNN, December 4, 2014. www.cnn.com.

58. Earl Ofari Hutchinson, "It's Time for Cops to Break the Blue Code of Silence," *The Blog*, HuffPost, September 25, 2016. www.huffingtonpost.com.

59. Hutchinson, "It's Time for Cops to Break the Blue Code of Silence."

60. Quoted in Annie Sweeney et al., "Top Cop Seeks to Fire 7 Officers for Lying About Laquan McDonald Shooting," *Chicago Tribune*, August 18, 2016. www.chicagotribune.com.

61. Quoted in Scott Daugherty, "Former Portsmouth Officer Stephen Rankin Guilty; Jury Recommends 2½ Years for Voluntary Manslaughter," *Virginian-Pilot* (Norfolk, VA), August 4, 2016. http://pilotonline.com.

62. Quoted in D.K., "What the Cops Say," *Policing in America* (blog), *Economist*, April 27, 2015. www.economist.com.

Chapter Five: Improving Policing, Strengthening Relationships

63. Quoted in Nicholas Phillips, "To Save Black Lives, Protester Bruce Franks Will Do the Unthinkable: Work with the Cops,"

St. Louis (MO) Riverfront Times, September 2, 2015. www.riverfronttimes.com.

64. Quoted in Phillips, "To Save Black Lives, Protester Bruce Franks Will Do the Unthinkable."

65. Quoted in Phillips, "To Save Black Lives, Protester Bruce Franks Will Do the Unthinkable."

66. Quoted in Phillips, "To Save Black Lives, Protester Bruce Franks Will Do the Unthinkable."

67. Brittany Packnett, interviewed by Audie Cornish, "Black Lives Matter Publishes 'Campaign Zero' Plan to Reduce Police Violence," NPR, August 26, 2015. www.npr.org.

68. Kim Covington, "6 Ways to Improve Police and Community Relations," AZCentral, September 21, 2015. www.azcentral.com.

69. Covington, "6 Ways to Improve Police and Community Relations."

70. Quoted in Libor Jany, "Minneapolis Police Reveal Changes to Use of Force Policy," *Minneapolis Star Tribune*, August 9, 2016. www.startribune.com.

71. Christopher I. Haugh, "How the Dallas Police Department Under David Brown Became a Model for Reform," *Atlantic*, July 9, 2016. www.theatlantic.com.

72. Quoted in Haugh, "How the Dallas Police Department Under David Brown Became a Model for Reform."

73. Quoted in Fox News, "Dallas' Top Cop Has Answer for Protesters: Join Us," July 11, 2016. www.foxnews.com.

74. Quoted in Mike Maciag, "Almost All Police Departments Plan to Use Body Cameras," *Governing*, January 26, 2016. www.governing.com.

FOR FURTHER RESEARCH

Books

Sue Bradford Edwards and Duchess Harris, *Black Lives Matter*. Minneapolis, MN: ABDO, 2016.

Marc Lamont Hill, *Nobody: Casualties of America's War on the Vulnerable, from Ferguson to Flint and Beyond*. New York: Atria, 2016.

Wesley Lowery, *They Can't Kill Us All*. New York: Little, Brown, 2016.

Kekla Magoon, *How It Went Down*. New York: Holt, 2014.

Mary Canty Merrill, *Why Black Lives Matter (Too)*. Bloomington, IN: AuthorHouse, 2016.

Peggy J. Parks, *How Prevalent Is Racism in Society?* San Diego, CA: ReferencePoint, 2015.

Internet Sources

Jerry Askin, "Teen Makes Documentary on Racial Profiling for National Contest," News Channel 10 (Amarillo, TX), July 7, 2016. www.newschannel10.com/story/32397126/teen-creates-documentary-on-racial-profiling-for-national-contest.

Lincoln Blades, "How Michael Brown's Death Awakened a Nation to Police Brutality," *Teen Vogue*, August 9, 2016. www.teenvogue.com/story/michael-brown-death-anniversary-police-brutality-black-lives-matter/amp.

Carolyn M. Brown, "11 Major Misconceptions About the Black Lives Matter Movement," *Black Enterprise*, July 16, 2016. www.blackenterprise.com/news/hot-topics/11-misconceptions-black-lives-matter-part-1.

Phil Helsel, "Twin Teens in Car When Jordan Edwards Killed by Cop Speak Out," NBC News, May 9, 2017. www.nbcnews.com

/news/us-news/twin-teens-car-when-jordan-edwards-killed-cop
-speak-out-n757081.

Wesley Lowery, "Black Lives Matter: Birth of a Movement," *Guardian* (Manchester), January 17, 2017. www.theguardian.com/us
-news/2017/jan/17/black-lives-matter-birth-of-a-movement.

Caleb Roberts, "Racial Profiling Raises Its Ugly Head (Again): A Night in the Life of a Black Man in Milwaukee," *Speak Freely* (blog), American Civil Liberties Union, February 22, 2017. www
.aclu.org/blog/speak-freely/racial-profiling-raises-its-ugly-head
-again-night-life-black-man-milwaukee.

Chelsea Stone, "This Teen Perfectly Summed Up the Black Lives Matter Movement in Class," *Teen Vogue*, September 28, 2016. www.teenvogue.com/story/teen-black-lives-matter-explanation
-viral-speech.

Danny Wicentowski, "Dorian Johnson: A Year After Mike Brown's Death, He's Still Grappling with the Fallout," *St. Louis (MO) Riverfront Times*, August 5, 2015. www.riverfronttimes.com/news
blog/2015/08/05/dorian-johnson-a-year-after-mike-browns
-death-hes-still-grappling-with-the-fallout.

Websites

American Civil Liberties Union (www.aclu.org). Working with courts, legislatures, and communities, the ACLU fights to defend and preserve the rights and liberties guaranteed for all citizens under the US Constitution. The website search engine produces numerous articles about racism and race-related topics, including many related to Black Lives Matter.

Anti-Racist Alliance (www.antiracistalliance.com). This grassroots organization works to achieve racial equality. Many articles and videos about racism-related topics are accessible through the website.

Black Lives Matter (http://blacklivesmatter.com). Black Lives Matter seeks to fight antiblack racism, spark dialogue among black people and their supporters, and encourage social action and engagement. The website provides tweets, statements by activists, and other writings.

Black Youth Project (www.blackyouthproject.com). This group seeks to enrich the lives of young African Americans by better understanding their culture, behavior, and decision making. The website provides research summaries, blogs about (and by) black youth, and a wide variety of news articles, including many related to Black Lives Matter.

INDEX

PICTURE CREDITS

ABOUT THE AUTHOR

Peggy J. Parks holds a bachelor of science degree from Aquinas College in Grand Rapids, Michigan, where she graduated magna cum laude. An author who has written dozens of educational books on a wide variety of topics for young adults and children, Parks lives in Muskegon, Michigan, a town she says inspires her writing because of its location on the shores of beautiful Lake Michigan.